HO 27

Dinosaurs

Dinosaurs

Written by Francis Davies

Illustrated by Gian Paulo Faleschini

Gareth Stevens Publishing
A WORLD ALMANAC EDUCATION GROUP COMPANY

For a free color catalog describing Gareth Stevens' list of high-quality books and multimedia programs, call 1-800-542-2595 (USA) or 1-800-461-9120 (Canada). Gareth Stevens Publishing's Fax: (414) 332-3567.

Gareth Stevens Publishing would like to thank Rolf Johnson of the Milwaukee Public Museum, Milwaukee, Wisconsin, for his kind and professional help with the information in this book.

Library of Congress Cataloging-in-Publication Data

Davies, Francis.
    Dinosaurs / by Francis Davies ; illustrated by Gian Paulo Faleschini.
       p. cm. -- (Nature's record-breakers)
    Summary: Provides an assortment of facts on dinosaurs including those science deems
the first feathered, the fastest runner, and the fiercest predator.
    Includes bibliographical references and index.
    ISBN 0-8368-2474-1 (lib. bdg.)
    1. Dinosaurs--Juvenile literature. [1. Dinosaurs--Miscellanea.] I. Faleschini, Gian Paulo, ill.
II. Title. III. Series.
QE861.5 .D38   2000
567.9--dc21   00-025037

This edition first published in 2000 by
Gareth Stevens Publishing
A World Almanac Education Group Company
330 West Olive Street, Suite 100
Milwaukee, Wisconsin 53212 USA

Original edition © 1999 by McRae Books Srl. First published in 1999 as *Dinosaurs*, with the series title *Blockbusters!*, by McRae Books Srl., via de' Rustici 5, Florence, Italy. This edition © 2000 by Gareth Stevens, Inc. Additional end matter © 2000 by Gareth Stevens, Inc.

Translated from Italian by Phil Goddard, in association with First Edition Translations, Cambridge
Designer: Marco Nardi
Layout: Ornello Fassio and Adriano Nardi
Gareth Stevens editors: Monica Rausch and Amy Bauman
Gareth Stevens designer: Joel Bucaro

Printed in the United States of America

1 2 3 4 5 6 7 8 9 04 03 02 01 00

Contents

Words that appear in the glossary are printed in **boldface** type
the first time they occur in the text.

Early Discoveries

Fossilized dinosaur footprints were first discovered in 1802 by Pliny Moody, a Connecticut farmer. He found the prints in rock slabs in his field. He described them as "the footprints of Noah's raven." In a Bible story, Noah sent this bird out of the ark to explore the world after the flood.

The word *dinosaur* was first used in 1842 by scientist Richard Owen. He studied dinosaur **fossils** and found that the animals were much larger than existing **reptiles**. He called them *Dinosauria*.

Richard Owen

The greatest disagreement among early dinosaur scientists was between Edward Cope and Othniel Marsh. From 1870 to 1890, they worked in the American West. They discovered dinosaur "graveyards." The men were both good at leading **excavations**, but they disliked each other.

Edward Drinker Cope

Fascinating Fact

In 1824, William Buckland published the first scientific description of a meat-eating dinosaur. Buckland studied the dinosaur's huge tooth, which he had found in England. Buckland named the dinosaur Megalosaurus.

The most expensive early scientific **expedition** was to Tendaguru, Tanzania, in 1907. The Berlin Academy of Sciences organized the expedition at a cost of about $93,000. Over 1,500 men spent three years excavating more than 276 tons (250 metric tons) of fossils.

➤ The most famous mistake was the first reconstruction of an Iguanodon. A **model** of it (*far right*), created in 1854, showed it walking on four legs instead of two, and its thumb was at the end of its snout.

Did you know?

Q. WHAT DOES THE WORD *DINOSAUR* MEAN?

A. *Dinosaur* comes from the Greek words *deinos*, meaning "terrible," and *sauria*, meaning "lizards." Scientists first thought dinosaurs were huge, **extinct** lizards.

Q. WHAT IS PALEONTOLOGY?

A. Paleontology is the science that studies fossils of plants and animals and tries to **reconstruct** the characteristics of these plants and animals.

Q. HOW DO WE KNOW SO MUCH ABOUT DINOSAURS?

A. Scientists use fossils to reconstruct the skeletons of dinosaurs. From this, scientists are able to suggest what dinosaurs looked like, how they lived, what they ate, and other interesting details.

Q. How does a fossil footprint form?

A. First, an animal or plant leaves its imprint, or mark, in soft mud or sand. This imprint then hardens and fills with **sediment**, forming a "fossil footprint." Many plant and animal parts can make imprints, including animals' skin and tails, plant leaves, and shells.

Q. How does a fossil form?

A. If an animal dies and is quickly covered in sediment, it sometimes **decomposes** very slowly. Over time, its flesh, skin, and bones (or leaves and branches with plants) are replaced by rock particles. Eventually, the sediment also turns into rock, encasing the fossilized animal. The most common fossils are of hard objects, such as shells, bones, and teeth, but fossils of eggs, leaves, stomach contents, and even droppings have been found.

Fossils and Models

◀ To create a skeleton, scientists put fossil bones together like a huge jigsaw puzzle. They measure the bones and look for joints and places where muscles were attached to find out where the bones fit. Scientists also study animals that are similar to dinosaurs, such as reptiles, to help them.

1. A dinosaur dies.

2. Its body is covered with sediment.

3. The bones turn into rock, or fossilize.

4. **Erosion** or people uncover the fossil.

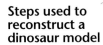

Steps used to reconstruct a dinosaur model

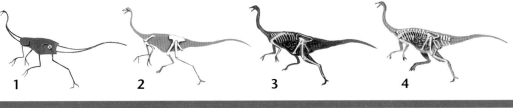

1   2   3   4

▲ To reconstruct a dinosaur, scientists first use a drawing to create a wire-frame model. They add plaster for muscle matter. Glass can be added for finishing touches.

◄ The most difficult stage of handling a fossil is removing it from the rock. This is done carefully using small picks, chisels, and brushes. At the museum, the fossil is cleaned using hand tools.

▲ Fossilized dinosaur eggs were first discovered in the Gobi Desert in Mongolia in 1923. Scientists found fossilized nests that were 100 million years old.

Fascinating Fact

Many dinosaur fossils come from "graveyards," such as the Dinosaur National Monument in Colorado, or nesting grounds, such as those in the Gobi Desert. A graveyard is a place where many animal fossils are found. A nesting ground is an area where groups of dinosaurs once laid their eggs. Fossilized nests and eggs can be found here.

How Did

Dinosaurs Live?

➤ Hadrosaurs, diplodocids, and camarasaurs were the best dinosaur parents. These animals built nests for their young. Fossilized trackways show that, while traveling, the larger animals often walked on the outside of the group. This suggests that the adults protected their young by keeping them in the middle.

Hadrosaurus

Fascinating Fact

Dinosaurs were first thought to be "terrible lizards." As more fossils were found, scientists realized that dinosaurs came in all shapes and sizes. They were covered in everything from scales to feathers to a bony, armorlike covering. Some had no covering at all! Some dinosaurs were **carnivores**, while others were **herbivores**. Some lived alone, and others lived in herds. Some thrived in cold areas, while others lived in warmer **climates**. Today's reptiles are nearly all carnivorous, scaly, **cold-blooded** animals. Some scientists suggest that dinosaurs were more closely related to birds or **mammals** than to reptiles. They believe that not all dinosaurs became extinct. Some simply **evolved** into birds.

Deinonychus was possibly the most **efficient predator**. This fast-moving dinosaur had a large brain. It may have been smart enough to hunt in groups. It used a long, sharp claw on its hind legs to slash enemies and prey.

The largest dinosaurs probably had an enlarged spinal cord.

Struthiomimus was probably the fastest runner. It may have reached speeds of up to 43 miles (70 kilometers) per hour. Its tail acted as a counterbalance to the weight of its long neck. This helped keep the animal's body stable when it ran.

Did you know?

Q. WHAT IS A PREDATOR?

A. A predator is an animal that hunts other animals for food. Predators often have certain features, such as speed, strength, and sharp teeth and claws. These features help the animal capture its **prey**.

Q. WHAT ARE CARNIVORES?

A. Carnivores are meat-eating animals.

Q. WHAT ARE HERBIVORES?

A. Herbivores are plant-eating animals. Their diet may include algae, fruit, flowers, and other plants.

Q. HOW DO WE KNOW THAT DINOSAURS LOOKED AFTER THEIR YOUNG?

A. Scientists have found fossilized remains of nests. There, adult animals cared for the young until they were old enough to take care of themselves.

The Dinosaur Family

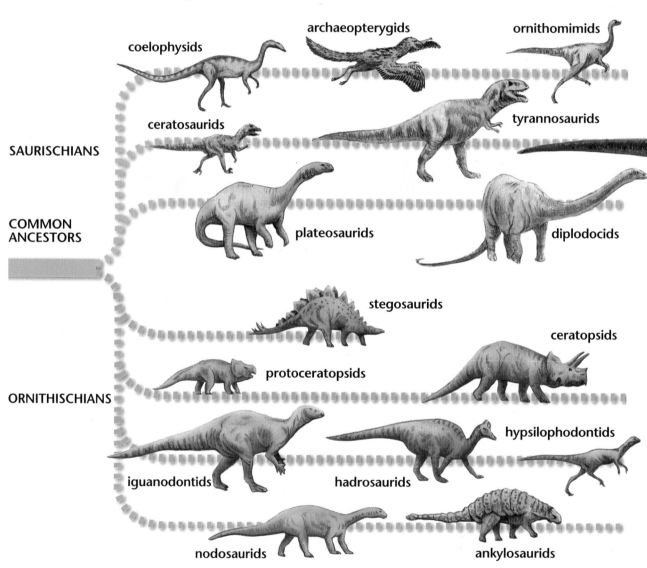

coelophysids

archaeopterygids

ornithomimids

SAURISCHIANS

ceratosaurids

tyrannosaurids

COMMON ANCESTORS

plateosaurids

diplodocids

stegosaurids

ceratopsids

protoceratopsids

ORNITHISCHIANS

hypsilophodontids

iguanodontids

hadrosaurids

nodosaurids

ankylosaurids

Dinosaurs are divided into two main groups: the saurischians and the ornithischians. The main difference between the two groups is in the structure of their **pelvis**. *Saurischia* means "lizard hips," while *Ornithischia* means "bird hips."

Spinosaurus

Fascinating Fact

Some dinosaurs could grow big, in part, because their legs grew straight down under their bodies, allowing their legs to support their weight. Most modern reptiles' legs are different.

present-day reptile (sand lizard)

ischium   **pubis**

Ornithischians had two bones in their pelvis pointing toward their tails. These animals were plant-eaters, or herbivores.

In saurischians, one pelvis bone, the ischium, faced backward. Another bone, the pubis, pointed forward.

ischium

pubis

Did you know?

Q. WHAT KIND OF ANIMALS WERE DINOSAURS?

A. Dinosaurs were **vertebrates**, meaning they had a backbone. They were probably reptiles, because they laid eggs and had a skull like a crocodile's. However, unlike many reptiles, scientists believe dinosaurs could walk, run, and jump, often using only their hind legs. Some scientists also believe that dinosaurs were warm-blooded, like today's birds and mammals. Modern reptiles are cold-blooded.

Q. WHAT IS THE PELVIS?

A. The pelvis is a bone structure that links the backbone, or spinal column, to the legs. A dinosaur's pelvis was very strong. Scientists believe this helped some dinosaurs run and jump using their hind legs.

13

Did you know?

Q. How are animals' teeth useful to scientists?

A. Teeth tell scientists about what an animal ate and what kind of life it led. Sharp teeth might mean that a dinosaur ate meat. An animal with large groups of teeth that were replaced by new ones probably ate tough, stringy plants and spent much of its time browsing. Soft but sharp teeth and a long muzzle could mean that an animal ate insects. An animal that had all these different types of teeth was probably a plant- and meat-eater, or **omnivore**, like humans.

teeth of an Iguanodon

Q. Were all reptiles dinosaurs?

A. No. During the Triassic period, a variety of nondinosaur reptiles existed, including those that lived in the sea or flew in the sky.

During the Triassic period, about 245 to 208 million years ago, the first sequoias and other conifers appeared. In areas where horsetails and ferns could no longer survive, cycads, ginkgoes, and yew trees began to grow. Changes in climate caused these changes in plant life.

▼ Saurischians called coelophysids were the first dinosaurs. They may have lived in herds. They were fierce predators and ate insects, amphibians, reptiles, and even other coelophysids! The smallest **species** was about as big as a chicken. The largest species grew to about 16 feet (5 meters) long, including the tail.

► Heterodontosaurs were one of the smallest dinosaurs of the Triassic period. Their name means "lizards with teeth of different shapes." They were the first ornithischians.

Triassic Period

Pangaea was the biggest continent ever. Its name means "all earth." During the Triassic period, all of Earth's land formed this single supercontinent.

Pangaea

➤ Teratosaurs and plateosaurs were the largest dinosaurs of the Triassic period. Teratosaurs were carnivores that weighed up to 1,544 pounds (700 kilograms) and grew as long as 20 feet (6 m). Plateosaurs were herbivores that walked on all fours. They grew to over 16 feet (5 m) long.

▼ Nothosaurs were unique marine reptiles. They had long bodies, the heads and tails of crocodiles, and finlike feet with small claws.

Fascinating Fact

During the Triassic period, many animal and plant species disappeared, but other species took their place. Scientists have found only a few fossils of small animals from this period. These animals had different types of teeth, large eyes, and short muzzles. One fossil is of a mouselike animal about 4 inches (10 centimeters) long. These were the first mammals.

➤ Mastodonsaurus was the largest amphibian that has ever lived.

Jurassic Period

During the Jurassic period, Pangaea split into two continents, Gondwana and Laurasia. Gondwana then split into huge pieces that formed South America, Africa, India, Australia, and Antarctica.

Laurasia

Gondwana

The first birds appeared during the Jurassic period. Flying animals also included pterosaurs, which had wings formed from membranes.

◀ Ceratosaurs were carnivores that lived during this period. They had cone-shaped teeth up to 2 inches (5 cm) long. The teeth grew one above the other, so new teeth quickly replaced worn-down teeth.

▼ Marine reptiles of this period included plesiosaurs with long necks and fins, icthyosaurs with dolphinlike bodies, and marine crocodiles with huge jaws.

◀ Allosaurs were the biggest carnivores of the Jurassic period. They grew up to 39 feet (12 m) in length and weighed as much as 5 tons (4.5 m tons). They had powerful arms and sharp claws.

➤ Ultrasaurus was the largest dinosaur. It lived during the Jurassic period and was up to 98 feet (30 m) long. It weighed more than a herd of 130 cows!

Fascinating Fact

During the Jurassic period, size became more important for survival. In battle, larger animals usually won over smaller animals. Both carnivores and herbivores, therefore, developed useful features through the process of evolution. Herbivores grew larger and developed spines and horns for protection. Carnivores grew larger and developed sharp claws and teeth.

Did you know?

Q. WERE CARNIVORES THE ONLY DINOSAURS ABLE TO GROW NEW TEETH TO REPLACE WORN ONES?

A. No, many herbivores also had this feature. Even today, some animals can "change" their teeth.

Q. WAS ULTRASAURUS THE ONLY GIANT DINOSAUR OF THE JURASSIC PERIOD?

A. No, many other very large herbivores existed during this period. Diplodocus was over 89 feet (27 m) in length, and some cetiosaurs grew to 72 feet (22 m) long.

Q. WHY DID STEGOSAURUS HAVE BONY PLATES ON ITS BACK?

A. Scientists think the plates may have helped the animal control its body temperature. The plates had blood vessels running through them. These vessels could have been used to get rid of body heat.

▲ Stegosaurs, or "covered lizards," were among the most well-armed herbivores. They were named for the plates on their backs. They also had powerful tails with long spikes.

Dinosaurs with

Feathers

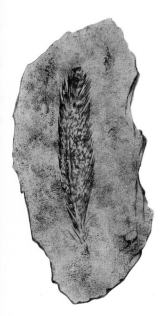

> Archaeopteryx was the first dinosaur to have feathers. It also had sharp teeth and claws, a long tail, and strong legs. Archaeopteryx lived during the Jurassic period. The first Archaeopteryx fossil, discovered in 1861, was a feather.

fossil of an Archaeopteryx feather

◄ Avimimus was probably the largest feathered dinosaur. It lived in the Late Cretaceous period. The ostrichlike Avimimus grew to 5 feet (1.5 m) in length. It could run fast, but it could not fly.

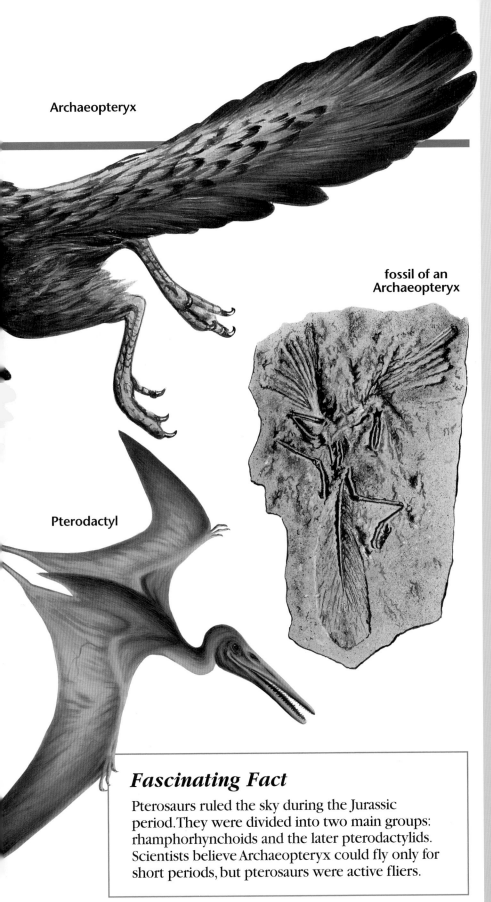

Archaeopteryx

fossil of an
Archaeopteryx

Pterodactyl

Did you know?

Q. **HOW DID FEATHERS COME INTO EXISTENCE?**

A. Scientists believe feathers are the result of a mutation, or change, in the process through which scales form.

Q. **WHY DID ANIMALS DEVELOP FEATHERS?**

A. Feathers are good protection against cold, heat, and dampness. Some scientists think this is why Archaeopteryx had feathers even before it could fly.

Q. **WAS ARCHAEOPTERYX THE ANCESTOR OF PRESENT-DAY BIRDS?**

A. Probably not. Its features are between those of an early dinosaur and a bird. Unlike today's birds, it had teeth and claws on its wings.

Fascinating Fact

Pterosaurs ruled the sky during the Jurassic period. They were divided into two main groups: rhamphorhynchoids and the later pterodactylids. Scientists believe Archaeopteryx could fly only for short periods, but pterosaurs were active fliers.

19

Cretaceous Period

A. Yes. The titanosaurs, or "titanic lizards," grew to 46 feet (14 m) long. The camarasaurs grew to 59 feet (18 m) in length and weighed as much as 22 tons (20 m tons).

Q. WHAT WAS THE PURPOSE OF THE "FRILL" AT THE BACK OF THE CERATOPSIAN'S HEAD?

A. A powerful set of jaw muscles was attached to this "frill." The ceratopsian had to have a strong jaw so it could chew tough plants.

Q. DID DINOSAURS BUILD NESTS DURING THE CRETACEOUS PERIOD?

A. Yes. Scientists have found nesting areas dating back to this period. These areas contained fossilized remains of hadrosaurs and Oviraptors. These animals protected their young by forming a circle around them and fighting off enemies with their horns.

▶ Hadrosaurs, or duck-billed dinosaurs, were some of the most unique Cretaceous dinosaurs. Some had growths like beaks on their foreheads or noses.

20

◀ The longest dinosaur tooth found is nearly 16 in. (40 cm) long.

During the Cretaceous period, about 144 to 65 million years ago, the continents broke away from Gondwana. The climate changed, and the environment became more varied. Many new dinosaur species developed.

Fascinating Fact

Scientists have no idea what colors dinosaurs were or what noises they made. The body of Tyrannosaurus suggests that it might have had a terrible roar. Some hadrosaurs had a nose like an elephant's trunk that may have been used to make noises. As for colors, if dinosaurs were like today's reptiles, they would have been greenish or brownish in color. This coloring would have helped the animal hide itself from its enemies. But it is also possible that their coloring was completely different!

▼ Dromaeosaurs were the fiercest predators of this time.

Life

Q. HOW DID THE RELATIONSHIP BETWEEN PLANTS AND INSECTS BEGIN?

A. During the Cretaceous period, some insects fed on magnolia flowers. As the insects — now covered in pollen — moved to other flowers, the insects **pollinated** them. As the interaction between insects and plants began, papyrus, palms, water-lillies, and grasses filled the landscape.

Q. WHAT REPTILES BESIDES DINOSAURS EXISTED DURING THE CRETACEOUS PERIOD?

A. Many water-dwelling reptiles, including fishlike icthyosaurs, long-necked plesiosaurs, and large-mouthed mosasaurs, lived during this period. Crocodiles, turtles, lizards, and the first snakes roamed Earth at this time, too.

◤ Baryonyx was the dinosaur scientists believe most likely to have been a fish-eater. Baryonyx lived during the Cretaceous period and had a long, flat head and 128 sharp teeth. It grew up to 33 feet (10 m) long and 13 feet (4 m) tall.

◤ Nodosaurs and ankylosaurs were the best-protected dinosaurs of this period. Their bodies were covered in bony plates.

Fascinating Fact

Some people believe that ancient water reptiles did not die out with the dinosaurs; instead, they are still living in deep oceans. For example, some people believe "Nessie," the famous "monster" of Loch Ness in Scotland, is a plesiosaur that was stranded there at the end of the Ice Age. No one, however, has proof that creatures like Nessie exist.

Magnolias were the first known flowering plants. They were followed by roses and trees with leaves that changed color with the seasons. These included birch trees, poplars, and oaks.

▶ Baryonyx had claws 1 foot (31 cm) long that may have been used for fishing.

▽ Pachycephalosaurus had one of the thickest skulls of any dinosaurs of this time. The top of its skull was over 10 inches (25 cm) thick.

◀ Mammals first appeared during the Jurassic period and continued to evolve during the Cretaceous period. Insect-eating mammals and marsupials appeared at this time. One marsupial, the opossum, was about the size of a rat and similar to its modern-day descendants.

Q. HOW DID TYRANNOSAURUS USE ITS ARMS?

A. Tyrannosaurus's arms were too short to reach its mouth, so it is not clear how the arms were used. They may have been used for balance. When the animal was moving, its tail helped balance the weight of its huge head and body. When it stood still or stretched, however, its arms would have provided a little extra balance.

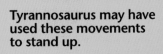

3

2

1

Tyrannosaurus may have used these movements to stand up.

Q. WHICH DINOSAUR HAD THE MOST TEETH?

A. Hadrosaurs had 200 to 400 teeth, with another 1,200 replacement teeth underneath. They used their teeth to grind the tough plants they ate.

Special

Dinosaurs

➤ Tyrannosaurus is the most famous dinosaur of all. It lived in the Cretaceous period and grew to 39 feet (12 m) long. It weighed over 7 tons (6 m tons) and had sawlike teeth 7 inches (18 cm) long. Since Tyrannosaurus was not the fastest or the deadliest of the dinosaurs, it may have fed on carrion, or dead animals.

Tyrannosaurus rex

◄ Iguanodon was the first dinosaur identified as an ancient herbivorous reptile. Fossils of it were found in Sussex, England, by a local doctor and his wife. Iguanodon was also the first dinosaur to have its lifestyle and habits studied and reconstructed. This Iguanodon skeleton (*left*) was built in 1878.

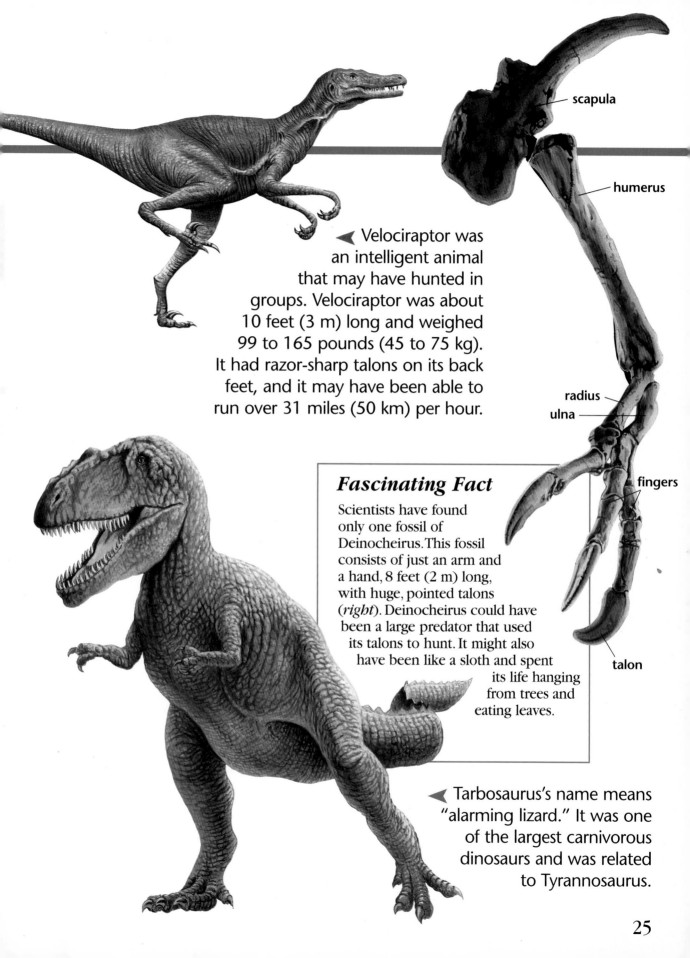

scapula

humerus

Velociraptor was an intelligent animal that may have hunted in groups. Velociraptor was about 10 feet (3 m) long and weighed 99 to 165 pounds (45 to 75 kg). It had razor-sharp talons on its back feet, and it may have been able to run over 31 miles (50 km) per hour.

radius

ulna

fingers

Fascinating Fact

Scientists have found only one fossil of Deinocheirus. This fossil consists of just an arm and a hand, 8 feet (2 m) long, with huge, pointed talons (*right*). Deinocheirus could have been a large predator that used its talons to hunt. It might also have been like a sloth and spent its life hanging from trees and eating leaves.

talon

Tarbosaurus's name means "alarming lizard." It was one of the largest carnivorous dinosaurs and was related to Tyrannosaurus.

Q. WHAT DOES EXTINCT MEAN?

A. An animal or plant is extinct when all examples of its species die out, or disappear from Earth. Scientists believe almost all Earth's dinosaurs became extinct 65 million years ago.

Q. HOW DO WE KNOW DINOSAURS BECAME EXTINCT IN THE CRETACEOUS PERIOD?

A. Layers of rock that formed after the Cretaceous period do not contain any dinosaur fossils. Many animal and plant species died out at the same time. In fact, about 75 percent of all life on Earth disappeared.

Q. HOW MANY THEORIES EXIST ABOUT WHY THE DINOSAURS BECAME EXTINCT?

A. Several different scientific theories exist. It is still difficult to explain why some species died out, while others did not.

Q. WHAT IS A METEORITE?

A. A meteorite is a piece of rock or metal from space that hits Earth.

Extinction

The most likely reason for the dinosaurs' disappearance was that Earth was hit by a large **meteorite** or asteroid. The impact would have caused huge explosions, strong winds, and great heat that could **vaporize** rock, water, and forests. For months, a huge cloud would have covered the planet, blocking the sun. First, the plants would have died, then the herbivores that fed on them, and finally the carnivores. In a short time, the entire climate would have changed, and most life would have been wiped out.

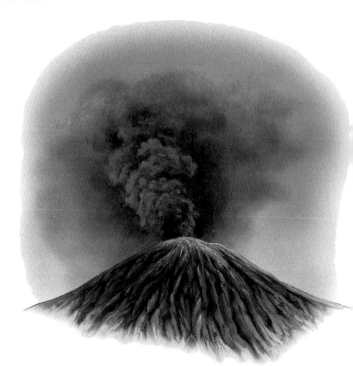

Some scientists believe dinosaurs died out after a volcanic eruption 65 million years ago. This was the worst eruption in Earth's history. It released huge amounts of carbon dioxide, acid, and ash into the air. Acid rain and lack of sunlight damaged the forests and changed the climate. This theory is the second most popular theory for the extinction of dinosaurs.

vaporized water

land destruction

earthquakes

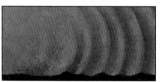

tidal waves

burning fires

ash and dust

acid rain

temperature changes

➤ A crater in the Gulf of Mexico region may have been created by a huge meteorite. The crater is about 124 miles (200 km) across.

Fascinating Fact

If a meteorite or asteroid would strike Earth again, it could wipe out thousands of species, including humans. To prevent this catastrophe, scientists have organized a series of projects, including Spacewatch and Project Itanet. These projects are designed to warn us of any dangerous objects coming toward Earth. Telescopes will constantly take photographs and alert us to any possible dangers.

Early rodents may have eaten dinosaur eggs.

◀ A much less likely possibility behind the dinosaurs' extinction: dinosaurs became prey to a new and powerful predator — mammals.

More Records

▶ Compared with its body size, Stegosaurus had the smallest brain of any animal that has ever lived. Its brain was about the size of a walnut. This herbivore also had weak teeth. It probably swallowed stones to grind food in its stomach.

Stegosaurus

▶ Diplodocus was one of the longest dinosaurs. It reached lengths of 89 feet (27 m).

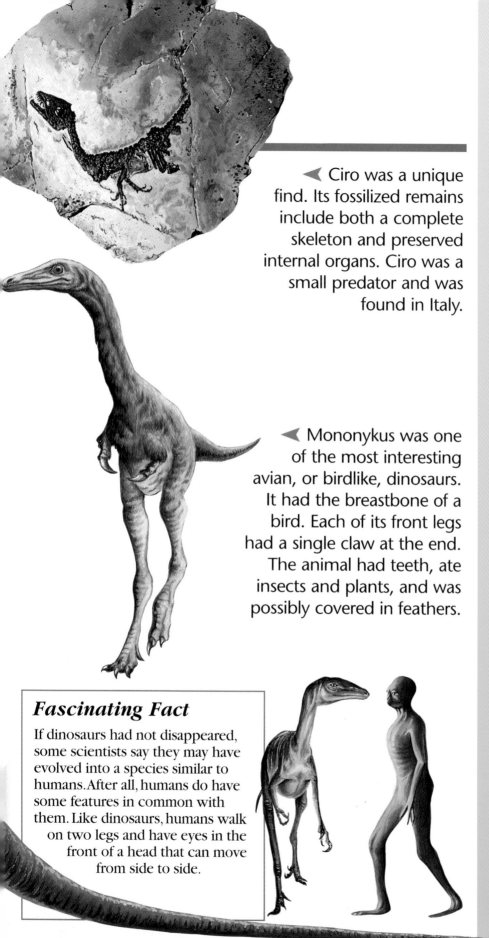

◀ Ciro was a unique find. Its fossilized remains include both a complete skeleton and preserved internal organs. Ciro was a small predator and was found in Italy.

◀ Mononykus was one of the most interesting avian, or birdlike, dinosaurs. It had the breastbone of a bird. Each of its front legs had a single claw at the end. The animal had teeth, ate insects and plants, and was possibly covered in feathers.

Fascinating Fact

If dinosaurs had not disappeared, some scientists say they may have evolved into a species similar to humans. After all, humans do have some features in common with them. Like dinosaurs, humans walk on two legs and have eyes in the front of a head that can move from side to side.

Did you know?

Q. DID ALL DINOSAURS DIE OUT 65 MILLION YEARS AGO?

A. Some scientists believe a few species survived after this time. They have found fossilized dinosaur bones dating later than the theoretical period of extinction. Scientists are still studying the bones because they could be older than the rocks in which they were found.

Q. DO SCIENTISTS COME UP WITH NEW THEORIES ABOUT DINOSAURS AS MORE FOSSILS ARE FOUND?

A. Yes. Most of what we know about dinosaurs has been learned in the last fifty years. New fossil finds and new ways of researching dinosaurs will provide more information about them.

Q. ARE PEOPLE STILL LOOKING FOR DINOSAUR FOSSILS?

A. Yes. Scientists are still conducting excavations, or digs. Places that once had fertile land, such as the Gobi Desert and the sub-Saharan area, are very good places to search.

Glossary

carnivores: animals that eat meat.

climate: the average weather conditions over a period of time. A desert, for example, receives very little rain and therefore has a dry climate.

cold-blooded: unable to control one's body temperature. Some cold-blooded animals, such as lizards, need heat from the sun or from other sources outside their bodies to keep warm.

decomposes: breaks down or decays.

efficient: productive without wasting energy.

erosion: the act of wearing away soil by wind, water, or glaciers.

evolve: to develop or change shape gradually over a long period of time.

excavation: the act of digging for and uncovering fossils.

expedition: a journey made for a certain reason, such as for an excavation.

extinct: no longer alive, such as when all the animals of one species die out.

fossils: traces or remains of animals or plants from an earlier period of time that are often found in rock.

herbivores: animals that eat plants.

mammals: warm-blooded animals that feed their babies on milk produced by the mother and usually give birth to live young.

meteorite: a piece of rock or other matter that falls from outer space and hits Earth.

model: a representation, or copy, of an object.

omnivore: an animal that eats both plants and meat.

paleontology: the study of plant and animal fossils to find out more about life in past geological time periods.

pelvis: the set of bones that links the spinal cord, or backbone, to the legs.

pollinate: to carry pollen from one plant to another, so the plants may reproduce.

predator: an animal that hunts and kills other animals for food.

prey: animals that are hunted and eaten by other animals.

reconstruct: to put together or build again.

reptiles: cold-blooded animals, such as snakes and lizards, that usually have scaly skin.

sediment: dust or dirt deposited by water, wind, or glaciers.

species: animals or plants that are closely related and often similar in behavior and appearance. Members of the same species can breed together.

theory: a scientific explanation for an event. It can be a guess that is based on available facts but cannot be proven true.

vaporize: using heat to change a material such as water into a vapor or gas.

vertebrate: an animal that has a backbone, or spinal column.

More Books to Read

American Museum of Natural History: On the Trail of Incredible Dinosaurs. William Lindsay (DK Publishing)

Did Dinosaurs Live in Your Backyard? Questions and Answers About Dinosaurs. Melvin Berger and Gilda Berger (Scholastic Reference)

Digging into Dinosaurs. Ranger Rick's Naturescope Guides. National Wildlife Federation (McGraw-Hill)

Dinosaurs: The Fastest, the Fiercest, the Most Amazing. Elizabeth MacLeod (Puffin)

Dinosaurs! Strange and Wonderful. Laurence Pringle (Penguin USA)

How to Draw Dinosaurs. Art Smart (series). Christine Smith (Gareth Stevens)

The New Dinosaur Collection (series). (Gareth Stevens)

Painting and Coloring Dinosaurs: Draw, Model, and Paint (series). Isidro Sánchez (Gareth Stevens)

World of Dinosaurs (series). Richard Grant (Gareth Stevens)

Videos

Dinosaur. (Dorling Kindersley)

Dinosaurs! Complete Set. (PBS Home Video)

National Geographic's Dinosaur Giants: Found. (National Geographic)

National Geographic's Really Wild Animals: Dinosaurs and Other Creature Features. (National Geographic)

Nova — Dinosaur Hunt. (WGBH Boston)

Web Sites

Discovery Channel Online: Fossil Zone
www.discovery.com/exp/fossilzone/fossilzone.html

Download a Dinosaur
www.rain.org/~philfear/download-a-dinosaur.html

San Diego Natural History Museum Kids' Habitat: Dinosaur Dig
www.sdnhm.org/kids/toc.html

Zoom Dinosaurs
www.EnchantedLearning.com/subjects/dinosaurs/

Some web sites stay current longer than others. For further web sites, use your search engines to locate the following keywords: *Cretaceous, dinosaur extinction, dinosaurs, fossils, Jurassic, paleontology, Triassic,* and *Tyrannosaurus rex.*

Index